Why Are They Like That? Women

Questions you've dared to ask, answered by real people, celebrities and experts

A book series based on the award-winning sharing project that's captured worldwide attention helping people in their personal, social and business relationships

Phillip J. Milano

For Robin, Jacob, Lucas and Ben

Publisher:
Y Forum
yforum@yforum.com

ISBN: 978-1-07-952986-9

Cover and interior layout by Sandy Weber,
Key 3 Creative, Jacksonville, Florida
Cover photo credit: Rawpixel. Stock photo for illustrative purposes only; any person depicted is a posed model.

Content based in part on the popular Y? sharing project and Dare to Ask column

Find out more about the author, upcoming books and speeches at www.phillipmilano.com, www.facebook.com/PhillipJMilano or @PhillipMilano.

Books In This Series

Why Are They Like That? Blacks

Why Are They Like That? Whites

Why Are They Like That? Hispanics

Why Are They Like That? Asians

Why Are They Like That? Gay Men

Why Are They Like That? Lesbians

Why Are They Like That? Women

Why Are They Like That? Men

Why Are They Like That? Rich and Poor

Why Are They Like That? Religious (or not)

Why Are They Like That? Disabled People

Why Are They Like That? Young and Old

Praise for the Y? sharing project and the book "I Can't Believe You Asked That!" (Perigee)

"Milano is quietly revolutionizing cross-cultural communication..."
- Pulitzer Prize-winning columnist Leonard Pitts

"If you've ever hesitated to ask a question because you think it might be considered insensitive or impolitic, now is your chance ... Nothing is considered out of bounds..."
- CNN Headline News

"(It) tells more about who we are and how we feel about each other than you're likely to learn from a dozen sociology texts…"
- Washington Post News Service

"Mr. Milano has dared to open the field of debate to the maximum…"
- Le Monde, Paris

"(A) remarkable contribution to cross-cultural understanding…"
- The (London) Guardian

"A truly rare achievement … has the potential to have a profound impact on the way we all see and understand each other..."
- Playboy magazine

"It's an incredible book. It diffuses everything ... Nothing is off limits, and the questions have that childlike honesty to them..."
- Dee Snider, Twisted Sister; host, "Dee Snider Radio"

"A take-no-prisoners attitude prevails between the volume's covers . . . This book is hard to put down..."
- Midwest Book Review

"A+ (highest rating) … Everything you wanted to know but were afraid to ask gets tackled here ..."
- Entertainment Weekly

CONTENTS

Introduction

Why Are They Like That? is a series of books based on an award-winning worldwide sharing project in which real people, experts and celebrities talk about things that make us different from each other. Silly things. Sad things. Funny things. Profound things.

Read with an open mind and we believe that by the time you're finished you'll have a much better understanding of how to make more and real friends, money and love. It's that simple.

Why? Because this isn't about trying to get ahead with diversity training. We are well beyond that. According to the Census Bureau, by 2050 the United States will have no racial or ethnic minority.

No, this is about moving past talking about how to understand each other to talking to each other. Right now.

That's why there's no agenda to these books other than getting the conversation going. We can discuss studies and methods for elevating social consciousness all we want, but there is no substitute for real dialogue.

That's where Why Are They Like That? stands apart from other books on the topic. You will see how people talk about their real differences of race, religion, sex, disability and more.

The success of the approach is proven: It's based on the ground-breaking Y? website project, blog and column that have attracted millions of visitors and worldwide media attention.

Our hope is that by reading, you will become more comfortable asking and answering the questions yourself, expecting the unexpected in return and helping change the ground rules for how we learn from and about each other. To that end, we wrap up each book in the series with our O.U.T.L.O.U.D. Method for Dialogue, with tips to help you get your own conversations started. Ultimately, that is what this effort is all about.

After all, if you want to make more friends, money and love, you better know the people you're talking to, selling to or opening to. Knowledge isn't just power. It's all power.

Enjoy.

Phillip J. Milano
Founder, Y?

And the sexiest age for a woman is…

They asked:

When is a woman at her sexiest in life?

Lauren, Australia

You said:

It's one thing to have a rifle. It's another to know how to pick off a deer at 200 yards. Older women who have mastered "the art" blow away the competition.

Adam, 42, Illinois

Some women are young and sexy. But some put on a few pounds in the right places and get a good streak of gray hair and age into their sexiness.

Amos, 32, Chicago

If you look at it biologically, a woman who is fertile is sexy. From that view, a woman is most desirable to a man at a younger age.

Cat, 20, female, Tampa

I can often look past the years to see, in many women, that lingering aura of the youthful beauty they once had. It may be in their eyes or smile, or the shape of their nose. Match that with their higher degree of wisdom and experience, and it is far sexier. But I would never have been able to think that way when I was 25.

Ardie, 54, Canada

I've met 40-year-olds with bodies teens envy, and teens with charm, wit and traveling experience in spades.

John, 24, Boynton Beach

Younger men are the ones attracted to me. … I'm very confident with my sexuality. I'm bolder and more assertive. And I don't feel my body or sex is all I have to offer.

T.M., 36, female, Indiana

It depends a bit on their ethnicity, too. The ones who look sexier in their 30s are Latins and sometimes Middle Easterners. The ones who look better in their mid-20s are East Indians, African descendants and Northern Europeans. The ones who look better in their early 20s or earlier are Native Americans and some Middle Easterners.

D-mike, 20, San Antonio

We found:

Sure, we've all heard of studies that say women are considered most attractive when they're young because men are yearning to reproduce, but that's more about old guys trying to regain their youth, said celebrity psychologist and sexpert Dorree Lynn (drdorree.com), author of "Sex for Grownups."

For a different position, let us travel back to the Europe of yore, when a young man was initiated into sexuality with an older, beautiful woman. Why? Maybe because society and the media weren't around saying if you "gain a few pounds, get a few edges and knotty bones and your butt droops" that you're past your prime, Lynn said.

"She was a woman of the world, and that was considered sexy and beautiful. ... The bottom line is that a woman is sexiest when she feels she is at her sexiest, not when her hormones peak. Attitude trumps technique."

In Lynn's studies, half of women said sex over 50 didn't exist, and half said the sex was the best. Ever.

So, sexiness is just how you look at yourself?

"It's being comfortable in your own skin," Lynn said. "Paris Hilton, Lindsay Lohan, Heidi Montag — whether it's boobs or nose or hair, it's always a new look. There's no beauty in that. Or sexiness."

Run to me, when you need ... a jerk

They asked:

Why do women always run to men who are assholes or abuse them?
And why can't they get out of these relationships?

Mike, 20, Iowa

You said:

Some find them "exciting." They like living on the edge. Some
think they can "save" the poor, misunderstood fellow. They
believe they're not really all that bad underneath, and they (the
woman) will uncover the good in them. The majority are simply
attracted to the men who are what they are used to; and, sadly, they
are used to abuse. I was once in that category.

Robin, 55, female, Westland, Mich.

Easy. When a girl dates a bad boy, it is obviously all on him. She is
always the blameless victim who gets sympathy and always has
entertaining drama stewing so she can be the center of attention
with her friends. If he dumps her, that's just the bum being the jerk
he is. Being with a nice guy has deep risks. If there are problems,
there's a good chance he isn't causing them. There is no drama to
passively be entertained by; she has to be her best self and bring
something to the table.

G.G., 45, male, Idaho

This applies to both genders. Some women are like assholes, and
for some reason, the abused men do not get out of the relationship.
Maybe he doesn't know better that there are good women out
there, too.

S.C., male, Texas

Some women have such low self-esteem that they think no man
would want them, so when one does show interest, they'd rather
take the abuse than be alone. And, as sick as it sounds, some
women believe jealousy and abuse prove the man cares about them.

M., female, Dallas, Ga.

We found:

Yes it's true: Some men like to get their bad self on, and too many women yearn to domesticate them, said Illinois therapist Kari Hunter (karihunter.com), who has spent more than two decades helping couples through relationship and marital woes.

"We can go back to a woman's childhood and their relationship with their father: Were they the apple of Dad's eye, or not?

Often, they're socialized to be maternal, to tame and shape in their relationships. Then they get excited by the bad boy, but eventually expect him to be other than what he is."

Then what do they do? Hit up a "nice-guy" male friend and cry on his shoulder.

It happens the other way around, too, but men aren't socialized to whine about it, lest they "look like a sap," Hunter said.

The media don't help, reinforcing flamboyant relationships with wild guys — witness the reinvention of Sherlock Holmes as a bad boy in the movie remakes with Robert Downey Jr. — but it's more fun to see that than an accountant and schoolteacher "just made for each other," she noted.

Ideally, women should have long-term relationship goals ... and take time between break-ups so they can start fresh with the right guy.

"They should follow advice Madonna doesn't seem to: Remember 'Don't settle for second-best, baby'?"

Don't always stamp a stigma on this "tramp" mark

They asked:

Why are tattoos on the lower backs of women called tramp stamps?

D., 53, female, Springtown, Texas

You said:

Because the tattoo is half above the pant line and half below. If the tattoo were completely covered, no one would notice it, and it wouldn't matter. If it were completely uncovered, people would think "that's cool" or "that person is socially deviant," depending on their view of tattoos. But since a tramp stamp is half uncovered, it makes people wonder what the other half looks like, and because of where it is located, that leads to other thoughts.

Kayla, 18, St. Augustine

Because of the type of women who usually get them.

A.L., 40, female, Kansas City, Mo.

It's my understanding when you hear the word "tramp," realistically you are probably referring to a female, right? So that's usually a woman's first place to put a tattoo. It's very easy to hide when it needs to be hidden. Also, I have yet to see a man with a tattoo right there. If so, I question his masculinity.

Lyrick, 20, female, Washington, D.C.

We found:

No shades of gray for Karen Hudson (tat2guru.com), author of "Living Canvas: Your Total Guide to Tattoos, Piercings, and Body Modification."

"I guarantee you that term was made up by some man who needs to be slapped upside the head," said Hudson. "A lot of men are threatened by women with strong sexual tendencies, who are confident and strong."

Hudson sees the "stamp" part of the pejorative as having come from early lower-back (or lumbar) tattoos that often featured simple tribal and Celtic designs that actually did look like stamps.

The "tramp" part came later, and now it's gone viral.

In an about.com essay, for example, Hudson laments the stereotypes of women with such tattoos, railing against a user's definition submitted to UrbanDictionary.com that reads, in part: "Those chicks with tramp stamps are the kinds of girls you take home to f-- . Don't get into relationships with them because they are often immature gold-digging sluts who sleep with everyone."

That's not to say some women aren't trying to convey a message, especially when such marks show a little and hide a little.

"It's a way to be suggestive and powerful without actually going the rest of the way," Hudson said. "And sexy. So is cleavage. But it doesn't mean she's inviting anyone."

After all, she said, some women are just comfortable being women.

"They don't mind having curves and accentuating that area, so they are more open, and if they are more open to something, maybe they are more open to others, but it doesn't make them a tramp."

Hudson, with lots of tatts herself, said she hasn't given over her lower back yet to the iron.

"I consider that prime real estate for a really amazing piece of artwork. At some point my entire back will be covered."

Poor guy: Can't catch a break with a rich gal?

They asked:

I don't have a glamorous job but enjoy it, and it pays my bills. Some women who caught my eye on a singles Web site are professionals. One asked what I do and hasn't talked to me since. Will "independent women" give lower-income guys a fair chance?

Dave, 26, Berea, S.C.

You said:

Most women want a man of means as much as most men want a woman who is physically attractive.

Lyddie, Chicago

I found that men who earn a lot less than I sometimes can't afford some events. If I pay, it throws the balance of power off.

Cassandra, 37, Chicago

I am a professional with a Ph.D. I married a "poor guy," and was that a mess. I prefer the men to be well-educated.

Leslie, 26, Tampa

I met my man when he was a cafeteria worker. My mom worries about us, but so far, so good. Problems may arise from lack of money, but ... it helps we are very easygoing and non-extravagant.

Natalia, 23, New York

Those women who see nothing wrong with looking down on your income (and yes, they're looking straight down at your poor butt) are probably the first to think it's awful guys want "hot" chicks.

Brian, 25, Indiana

We found:

Sociologist Christine Whelan (christinewhelan.com), who's written books on relationships like "Marry Smart: The Intelligent Woman's

Guide to True Love," commissioned a Harris survey of high-achieving men and women.

It found that a third of the women married someone who didn't earn as much as they did, and 67 percent would be comfortable as the primary earner.

Nowadays, there are more independent women, and they can choose whether they want a similar mate, said Whelan, a professor at the University of Pittsburgh.

"Potentially, more women earn a good income and see it as a freeing thing. They can marry for love. The flip-side is plenty of them say no, I'm educated and can make a good living, but I don't always want to have to."

Often it's not salary but education, social class or willingness to toss out gender roles that's vital. Education and upbringing give us a particular way of seeing the world, which usually is at the heart of long-term compatibility, Whelan said.

"Sex and passion only last so long; then you have to talk to someone at the end of the day," she said. "For example, on 'Family Guy' they were having a fight over a trivia question, and the guy said, 'You don't know that? The cat would know that answer.' And she said, 'Not everyone went to college.' It shows the fights you can have ... that can end up with one person sleeping on the couch."

Have you seen Jr.? Not after a woman's name

They asked:

Why don't more women name their children after themselves, and why aren't there more women with "Jr." after their names, like men?

Steve, Jacksonville

You said:

I think this relates back to the tradition of a family business or trade — where a father passes the business on to his son. Many businesses were named "Johnson and Sons," etc. I'm presuming that the practice of naming the son the same as the father also come from this practice.

Paula, 40, Wellington, New Zealand

Society still expects that women will give up their so-called "maiden" name for that of the husband, which would nullify the reason for having the suffix in the first place.

Mara, Dallas, Ga.

I was named for my mom (first and middle name), and it turned out to be a headache. ... I took a nickname when my mom and I worked at the same business, but my legal name stayed the same. At one point, we lived at the same address, worked at the same business and had the same name, so when we checked out our credit history, my mom had two of every credit card, and I had no credit history!

Anne, 49, Indianapolis

We found:

According to behindthename.com, "Jr." distinguishes a son with the same name from his father. He must be a son (not grandson), has to have the same middle name and Dad must still be alive. If you've got the same name as your grandpa, you use "II" after your name.

We always wondered if Bacon Cheeseburger Jr.'s dad was still alive, and now we know. Even though some twit at Wendy's always screws up and puts the "Jr." before "Bacon Cheeseburger" on the drive-through menu.

As far as why there aren't a lot of girl "Jrs.," Megan Smolenyak Smolenyak (megansmolenyak.com), chief family historian for Ancestry.com, said that back in the day, say in the 1700s or earlier, women were invisible in town records, mainly because they didn't own property.

So for men, there was a natural progression — hey, wait a second, you joker. You've got a squared last name.

"I'm a Smolenyak by birth and marriage," she said, "and since most professional genealogists use their full name, I didn't want to be too timid to use my full name."

Still kind of tricky. But anyway, for men, there was a progression toward using Jr. to distinguish a son from a father with the same name, in case the father passed property down to the son and it needed to be clear in probate and deed records just who was who.

And the reason these kids had the same name as their dad in the first place?

"It was tradition to name your child after yourself back then, as a way of preserving the family name and honoring those who came before," Smolenyak Smolenyak said. "It was habit."

She doubts Jr. will ever become popular for girls now that women own things, because people are now more into giving their offspring unique names.

"We're more creative these days," she said. Doubly so.

Some cleave to this locale to put their stash

They asked:

When I go out to a nightclub dancing, I carry my change purse and cell phone inside my bra cup. I can lock my pocketbook in the car and not have to worry about losing anything. A few people said I look cheap when I reach into my dress to get at my money. It hurt my feelings. If you're a woman who does this, what reaction have you had? I do this often and never lost anything. It works on my end.

Linda, 50, Boston

You said:

If it was good enough for Mae West, it's good enough for anyone.

Hope, 38, Pittsburgh

You must be a heavy gal for that to even work. I think it's pretty white trash to go digging in your underwear to tip the valet. Besides, YOU'RE 50! What nightclubs and dancing are you involved in? The behavior might be acceptable to someone in her early 20s. A middle-aged woman should have more class.

Dot, Los Angeles

We found:

Cue the stiff announcer in the tinny-sounding high school etiquette film: "And for our female students, remember, at age 25, it begins to look skanky to plunge your hand into your cleavage for cash. Before that age, however, boys will find this empowering activity a sign of independence. What's tha? (sound of vibrating ring tone) … is that your modern smartphone alerting you to a friend or extended warranty salesman? No need to keep them waiting. Get in there and dig around."

We'll let Susan Huston unearth some truth nuggets for us. She's an etiquette and fashion expert with more than three decades'

18

experience (SusanHuston.com), advises celebrities and Miss America contestants and has been interviewed by all sorts of media. Maybe not about bra-diving, but about other stuff.

In this day and age of lax decorum, some girls and women may need some training about their bras, she said (note with humor our use of "training" and "bra" in the same sentence).

"This is a habit some women got into back in the grandma days, when they had a hanky in their bosom," Huston said. "It can be difficult to break. If I could invent something fashionable to use instead of the bosom, I could be a millionaire."

But it does look pretty cheap to do that, she added, whether in a club or on a job interview, so for those women who actually don't know this: Don't do it!

"Women need to stop and think, your breast is part of you ... it might be seen as an open invitation. Women might think it's OK for convenience sake, but it doesn't appear that way. And so conflicts can arise."

And especially in an era of camera phones and social networking sites, what you do may be seen by millions, so be forewarned, she said.

"With women, it's about protecting their reputation. Maybe a man can still get away with a little scratching ... but with a woman, people seem to take it more seriously, and it's more noticeable, too. It's right in your face."

Her solution? Put the cash, plastic and lipstick in a small pocketbook with a long strap. Then there's no need for a multi-tasking bra.

Do dads spend enough time with their daughters?

They asked:

What do women think about their relationship with their fathers growing up, specifically how much time you needed to see them? Would weekends and a kiss at night have been enough for you?

Nick, 37, Australia

You said:

No! A girl learns what she wants out of a man from her dad. My dad was often on business from before school until evening, and when he did see me, he was tired or stressed. On the flip side, if you do only see a child on the weekends, you can't just be their "friend" ... they need a real father, not a buddy.

Anne, 49, Indianapolis

I still spend time with my dad. As the provider, we knew he was busy and stressed, but it didn't stop him from spending time with us on weekends. He put us to bed, and I can still remember him taking the time to blow-dry my hair just the way I wanted it, or later on as a teenager the conversations we had. ... As a result of the closeness we have, I can talk to or come to my parents with anything.

Serilda, 31, Jacksonville

Dad time is always good. I grew up in a happy, two-parent home but still remember that my dad and I walked to Donutland every Saturday morning; he'd drink coffee with a cherry doughnut and I got chocolate chip. We read the paper together. I appreciate my dad and the pressures upon him more each day.

A.C., 24, Iowa City, Iowa

We found:

Dads and daughters, read this and get bonding:

Quality and quantity of time together are important.

"So much of imprinting of children goes on in day-to-day living," said family therapist Beth Erickson (drbetherickson.blogspot.com), author of "Longing for Dad: Father Loss and Its Impact." "If Dad's not there when she's disappointed over her first love, that's hard to re-create once the tears have passed."

Girls often blame themselves for an absentee dad.

"Women are socialized that their success arena is in relationships," she said.

As a result, things can get screwy for a girl while dating or during marriage.

"They can carry this 'not good enough' mantle the rest of their lives, unless a psychotherapist helps them correct it," Erickson said. "There's a sense of unworthiness, no matter how many times someone tells you you're loved. ... In extreme cases she'll prove herself unworthy by having affairs."

Girls learn how to relate to men by how they relate to their father. Dads also provide encouragement.

"His job is to be a safe male for her to experiment with her femininity ... to learn she can be admired by a man without it boiling down to sex," Erickson said. "Dad also tells her, for example, if she's climbing a tree, to see how high she can climb."

Dads: If you can't always be there because of a job or other reason, explain why.

"Make sure the kids know it doesn't mean you don't love them. In the meantime, do things like leave Sticky notes that say 'I love you' or 'I'll miss you today.' And try to be there when you are there. Play Scrabble, or sit and talk with them. For girls, it can protect them from blaming themselves."

Nothing like a nice, clean-shaved toe

They asked:

Is it worth shaving my toes for the next 40 years of my life, or do people even notice?

Faye, 17, St. Louis

You said:

People don't notice. Don't bother.

Ellen, 47, Mesa, Ariz.

I also have hairy toes. I shave them; it only takes like three seconds to do it. I don't do it all the time, usually once every other week or so in the summer and less often in the winter.

Trisha H., 27, Flint, Mich.

We found:

After more than 50,000 submissions to the Y? sharing project, we can safely say we have now received the most inane, intellect-free, idiotic contribution yet. All in just five little words.

"People don't notice. Don't bother."

Oh ... Our ... God. And if you don't understand what we mean — hello, it means OMG but then substitute an O for one of the letters.

Someone is telling us that during these times we're in, people aren't all looking closely at the hairiness of each other's lowest extremities? Right.

"I would say in a heart-to-heart to this girl that life is too short to worry about it," said beauty-consultant-to-the-stars Noreen Young (noreenyoung.com). "Look what's happening in the world, and we're worrying about hair on our toes."

Oh.

But Young did say that if this girl lives in a place such as sunshiny Florida and if she wears sandals a lot and if it really bothers her ...

"You know, if it's to the point she feels she can braid it, she might want to do something about it. ... She may want to look her finger-licking best, or in this case toe-licking best," said Young, an internationally known makeup artist whose clients include Dennis Miller, Al Michaels, Chris Evert and the Nancy Grace show.

"It's like a woman in corporate America and all of sudden she's getting a little bit extra above the lip and doesn't want to look like a manny-girl."

So, for the toes, just shave them. No laser treatments, electrolysis, chemical depilatories, waxing or sugaring needed, Young said. A Ladies Bic will do. (Impressed by that list? We didn't even get into threading, an ancient Middle East form of hair removal that can work on toe and other hairs. Be warned: one Web site says "remember that threading is an intricate art that must be performed only by a skilled practitioner, and that it takes months to achieve proficiency. Nothing is more painful than threading performed by an inexpert hand." Owie.)

Young lamented a fairly sad state of current affairs in which many people, and especially teens and young adults, seem OK with coughing up hairballs of money to "perfect" their appearance.

"The media and ads play a role," she said. "You have this beauty trend with teens wanting to remove unwanted body hair. They are shaving not only their arms, but men are shaving their chests, getting waxed and also shaving 'down that way.' Girls, too.

"I wish I knew why, but I guess they equate it with a more clean, streamlined look, and they just have to do it."

Baring all about doing porn

They asked:

What encourages people to be porn actors or actresses?

Azucena, 30, female, London

You said:

For guys, it's pretty much what you may have already guessed.

Taz, 32, male, Detroit

Easy money. And lots of it.

Kelly, 19, Richmond, Va.

Although I can't say from experience, most women in that business have been sexually abused at a young age and haven't gotten counseling, so they act out sexually.

V., 20, female, Virginia

I work in a legal brothel and have asked that question to some of our ladies, several of whom have done porn. ... They generally enjoy the work, and with proper savings and investment can expect retirement within three to five years.

Tony, 45, Nevada

I had a roommate who had been a porn star, and I have several acquaintances who were strippers, and what most had in common was an array of psychological disorders from massive childhood abuse such that they were unable to hold down straight jobs.

Katrina, 43, Beverly Hills, Calif.

I've watched more porn flicks than I'd like to admit. I think a few of the most beautiful stars do it because they get paid well and hope it makes them stars in non-porn flicks. I think the majority are ruthlessly exploited.

Mike, 58, Evansville, Ind.

We found:

We thought about talking to the adult king himself, Ron Jeremy, but apparently he likes to get paid for his interviews.

So it was on to Leihla Leionni of Tampa, who pretty much got the ball rolling several years back on her 18th birthday, when a guy in a bar gave her his card and said to give him a call. She's done work for Demon Seed Pictures and Girls Gone Wild, and also been in numerous videos with names related to hands, mouths, faces and other body parts.

Various studies have reported that sex workers can suffer unusual stress from the rigors and stigma of their jobs, and that prior abuse can play a role in their career choice.

Leionni was having none of it, at least for herself and those she's worked with (not that we thought she'd agree).

"It's not true — I had a great childhood and loving parents who took care of me and got me what I wanted," she said. "I mean, I even had a pony, you know what I mean?"

So, then, reveal all. Why do it?

"I don't let others' opinions influence me, and I'm willing to try anything once. Other people said it was a horrible idea, but I had fun and didn't get ripped off," she said. "Ever since that first shoot, it's been exciting, and the money's good [$1,000 or so for three to four hours' work, up to $10,000 for a private video]."

But what about the folks?

"My mom was a little upset, but once she realized I was happy and making money, that was over real quick.

"And with my dad, we have sort of an unspoken agreement. I know he knows."

They call it girl talk ... and talk, and talk, and talk

They asked:

I still don't understand why women talk so damn much! Most of the time, they're talking about b- s-! Shoes, the mall, babies, clothes, makeup, celebrities, etc. Why is it I never hear women talking about anything deep?

David, Woodbridge, N.J.

You said:

You mean as opposed to talking about sports, how drunk they got last weekend, who they fucked while drunk, and what tools or toys they're going to buy?

A., 40, female, Missouri

If you choose to hang with bimbos, you're going to get blather about shoes and celebrities. Go to a Mensa meeting, join a book club or sign into a chat room about politics. ... Too many guys want little girls or subservient housewife types.

Dot, female, California

Roughly half the members of the Y? sharing project are women. So I would hardly say women "never talk about anything deep." And if women talk as much as you say, then they are bound to talk about things in-depth.

Carrie, 21, Houston

We found:

We tried to gab with a couple of well-known women who study how the sexes communicate, but their female publicists prattled on and on to us about how they were too busy working on new books (actually, they politely and quickly ditched us by e-mail, but we're still silently sulking alone).

26

One, Louann Brizendine (drlouann.com), clinical professor of psychiatry at the University of California San Francisco, wrote "The Female Brain," which repeated the oft-repeated claim that women average 20,000 words per day compared to men's 7,000.

That idea was highly criticized for not being backed with hard science, and other researchers have documented many studies, including at the University of Arizona and Washington University in St. Louis, that show men talk as much or more than women, depending on the situation.

What most experts seem to agree on is that there may be differences in why men and women communicate, if not how much they communicate. It's the classic idea that men reserve conversation to pass along knowledge and solutions, and women use it more to be supportive and social, said Scott Haltzman (drscott.com), a former Brown University professor of psychiatry and author of "The Secrets of Happily Married Women."

Research supports that "when men are stressed, they tend to close themselves off, while women tend to engage in more emotional connection," said Haltzman, who now is in practice in Florida at The David Lawrence Center. "As [researcher Deborah] Tannen says, women talk for rapport, men talk to report."

For women who complain their spouses don't listen, Haltzman suggests offering dialogue as a "task" rather than to bond.

"In general, keep things short, particularly if it's something you want him to help you with," he said. "If you want him to listen, speak in a way that he understands, instead of trying to get him to morph into Hugh Grant."

After the baby, can a woman's body snap back?

They asked:

I have a 1-year-old son and am having the worst time getting over the way my body looks. I have stretch marks, and my tummy is shaped different. I just can't get myself to love my body. Any advice?

Jessica, 19, Louisville, Ky.

You said:

You can find people who regard stretch marks as sexy.

Craig, Missouri

Eat right. Exercise at least three days a week. I don't buy the whole "accepting your body for what it is" approach.

Austin, 31, Frankfort, Ky.

I had a girlfriend whose husband left her when her tummy started to show, citing that she no longer turned him on. He is a scumbag and an embarrassment to men.

U., 29, male, Las Vegas

I've had six children. My breasts got all droopy and saggy — that bummed me out, as I don't feel as sexy as I used to. Cheer up, sweetie: Find friends to talk to in the same boat.

Rose, Pflugerville, Texas

The stretch marks are badges of honor — not evil things.

Sheila, 38, Tucson, Ariz.

The whole "get over it" comments — yeah right! It's hard to get over.

Susan, 21, Livonia, Mich.

Look at yourself in the mirror naked to begin to accept the way you look right now.

Suzette, 32, Saline, Mich.

If you want your figure back badly enough, you'll work for it.

Megan, 25, Niles, Mich.

Your son needs a mom with a good head on her shoulders to raise him, not a Barbie doll.

T., male, 17, Arizona

We found:

Ah, to be 19 and a young mother again.

Oh yeah. Forgot.

But those who can have a baby need not have a cow later about their looks. Ann Douglas (anndouglas.ca), author of "The Mother of All Pregnancy Books" series, said to consider the following about:

Stretch marks: Oils, butters and vitamin E aren't proven, so you may have to live with them. "Some of us are given genetically stretchy skin, but a lot aren't . . . the good news is they don't look like red crayon marks forever. They fade."

Weight: Talk to your doctor about healthful dieting. Remember that your body wants to store fat to prepare for a possible next pregnancy, so it might be working against you.

"Sometimes we have a sense that everyone has a perfect life and is wearing jeans after six weeks - and whoever made that up is lying."

Society: "People can be too judgmental. I'm not saying we need to go back to A-frame tent dresses, but now we feel we have to have our belly on display all the time . . . you're trying to enjoy a cone, and someone's looking at your stretch marks, and you're like, 'Hey this isn't causing the stretch marks, you want to wear this cone?' "

Getting too down: Don't panic or go it alone. "If you're really depressed, maybe see a therapist - it might be post-partum depression. It might be about more than just stretch marks. Once you're feeling better, you won't fixate on those."

If his fantasy ends up being about you

They asked:

Girls, if you found out a guy you knew fantasized about you, would you be offended, disgusted, intrigued, flattered, don't want to know, etc.?

Jayarby, 55, male, Philadelphia

You said:

I think it would be flattering. Maybe I'm fantasizing about him, too.

Jesse, 25, New Orleans

Sex is a private matter. Just as I don't go around talking about what my wife and I did when we made love the last time, I don't think it's appropriate to discuss what you do [in private] — unless such discussion is for a medical/therapeutic nature. I also think it would be disrespectful to my wife for the guy to even want to tell me.

S.R., 49, bisexual female, New Alexandria, Pa.

We found:

We thought and thought about whether we should feature this question, then put it out of our minds, then thought about it some more, then felt weird about it, then couldn't help ourselves from focusing on it, then felt slightly guilty, then kept dwelling on it, then stopped, then were dangerously inattentive in traffic, then felt the need for counseling.

So it was time to ring up Wendy Maltz, a sex therapist and co-author of "Private Thoughts: Exploring the Power of Women's Sexual Fantasies." Her Web site is www.HealthySex.com.

Basically, she says a girl's reaction to finding out a dude fantasizes about her depends on: the nature of her relationship to the dude (co-worker, friend or car mechanic?); whether she likes the dude; the status of both parties (single, dating someone, or married?); and how she found out.

"In general, I think if she didn't know the person well, a woman would be pretty suspicious about this . . . it's a very private thing to share. There's a sense of breaking through a social etiquette or barrier, and it could be interpreted as sexual harassment [at work]."

However, it's often the circumstances that govern the reaction:

"For example, if you heard through the grapevine that someone fantasized about you, it's more like finding out they have a sexual interest in you," Maltz said. "The question [above] implies that the fantasizing is more than a burp or onetime thing, which is like hearing that someone finds you hot. It would again depend on if she's attracted to the guy. It could be creepy if she finds him creepy in general."

Research shows that men's fantasies are often more visual, explicit and related to specific acts and body parts, while women's are typically more sensually oriented and focused on relationship dynamics — although more young women are now having "hotter" fantasies driven by a culture that offers up more sexually graphic images, Maltz said.

In a porn-saturated world where women are often objectified, they can be wary of any man fantasizing or gawking, she added. But knowing the person, feeling safe about them and being in an appropriate situation make a difference.

"Females who feel confident about themselves sexually may say, 'Cool, someone thinks I'm hot — I hope you enjoyed yourself.' "

This girl is ready to pack on some pounds

They asked:

I am small (125 pounds and 5 feet 7). To some this is ideal, but to me it is depressing. I've even stopped going to clubs, social functions and some of my children's activities. Any suggestions on how to gain weight?

T-C, 38, female, Seattle

You said:

The hell if you do! Lift weights or something to firm up if you're stressed, but don't get fat. It's B.S. when people say they like a big woman.

John, 47, Federal Way, Wash.

I'm 24, 5 feet 2, small-framed and eternally stuck at 95 pounds. I'm forever trying to gain weight. I also have a very fast metabolism. I understand what you mean.

Ashley, 24, St. Augustine

Maybe you feel bad because of cultural ideals of beauty. Sometimes I feel bad because I'm not curvy like the Mexican ideal (I'm Chicana). Make sure you are eating enough each day and getting good nutrition. [Also] martial arts bulks up your thighs and arms, while ballet makes your legs and butt bigger.

Diana, 18, Sacramento, Calif.

I once asked an overbearing pastor who squeezed my arm as if testing a side of beef and commented on my lack of "meat," why he didn't tell a fat person they were sooo chubby while giving them a poke like the Pillsbury Doughboy. That sure stopped his commentary.

Marlene, 50, Gillett, Penn.

My proportions are almost the same as yours, and I'm convinced I need to lose 10 pounds.

S.R., 23, female, San Antonio, Texas

As long as you're healthy, you're blessed and exactly where you need to be.

Kimberly, Austin, Texas

We found:

We almost choked on the defibrillator-size slab of tiramisu we were eating when we heard this. People upset with being too thin?

Before we have to eat our words . . .

Most female body-image issues related to being thin aren't really about being "too skinny," but about trying to hold to a Western standard of "curves," said Kathy Kater, a licensed independent clinical social worker who runs BodyImageHealth.org.

"It's as though women have to be perfect . . . have the breasts, the hips, a nice curve — but yet be thin, too," she said. "We're taught that if you don't have the body you want, you must be doing something wrong. [But] there are limits to the healthy ways we can influence our body shape."

It's possible T-C has Body Dysmorphic Disorder, an all-consuming obsession with the body or parts of it that a person has decided are intolerable.

"You end up spending time and energy on it to the point of it interfering with your otherwise normal daily life," said Kater, author of such popular books as "Healthy Bodies: Teaching Kids What They Need to Know."

Psychotherapy and medication can help.

While thin men can suffer ridicule because of stereotypes about masculinity, studies show most people who see a thin woman — even one without curves — assume she is happy, healthy and popular.

"If anything, the stereotypes for [thin] women are positive, not negative," Kater said.

Teed off at slow ladies on the golf course

They asked:

Do women really play golf slower than men?

R.M., male, Jacksonville

You said:

I think women tend to see a round of golf as a social occasion. . . . But that doesn't mean they're slower when it comes to actually getting to their ball and hitting the shots.

J.L., male, Ponte Vedra Beach

Here on the private courses, women do not play golf slower than men. On public courses, they are more likely to play slower than men because of their lower skill levels and the fact that many hit a shorter ball.

N.M., 85, male, Florida

Although women don't hit the ball as far, they also don't hit as far off the fairway.

Barb, Phoenix

They're slower because they have a lot of conversation while they're playing.

Luke, male, Los Angeles

Women don't play any slower than the men here. I think there are just a lot of grumpy old men who just have it in their heads that it is a man's game and that women don't belong on the golf course.

Gordon, 72, Sun City West, Ariz.

We found:

Do women mistake tee time for tea time? (Hey! Who just hit into us? Get a ranger!)

Time for a formal audience with "The Pope of Slope," Dean Knuth (popeofslope.com), the main developer of the USGA's Course Rating and Slope Rating System used throughout the world today, and creator of the U.S. Golf Association's "Pace Rating System" manual. Knuth, Golf Digest Contributing Editor, is known as the Tiger Woods of number-crunching in golf.

The "hit and giggle" golf myth about women really is just that, says the handicapping swami.

"The average women's handicap is about 14 shots higher than men in the U.S. . . . but women are more conscious of golf rules," he said. Since about 75 percent of U.S. golfers are men, "odds-wise there are more slower men's groups."

Cathy Harbin, vice president of golf revenue for Dallas-based private golf club operator ClubCorp, agrees women really do pay attention to the rules and pace of play.

"The universal fear is that women golfers, because they don't hit as far, will play slower. But in my experience that's proven not to be true," said Harbin, former general manager of The Slammer & Squire courses at the World Golf Village in St. Augustine, Fla.

Some men, however . . .

"They watch golf on TV. They watch guys study a shot, back off it, study again . . . they get in that mind-set."

For example, at a tourney at the World Golf Village, "I put the women out front. . . . the guys were like 'I can't believe it.' But they [stayed] at least a hole and a half ahead the entire day.

"There's a stigma, and [women] don't want to live up to it. So they say 'We'll be the opposite. We'll leave them in our dust.' "

The biggest cause of slow play? "Overloading the course," said Knuth. "That's a management issue."

Giving a French prostitute an Eiffel?

They asked:

What does it mean when an American calls someone a "French whore"?

Julie, 22, Nashville

You said:

Our country is still obsessed with moralistic rules and judges the way France glorifies the female body as immoral. These same people also don't want to admit that the American media glorifies the female body, too (but the plastic Barbie woman, not the real thing) — the same way they don't think of prostitution as an issue here.

Jessica K., 22, Huntsville, Texas

Simple: Like the average French person, whores over there have more elegance and class than their American colleagues.

Hanna, 27, Sweden

It's "You smell like a French whore" and refers to overindulgence in perfume. "Whore" would also indicate someone of a lower class putting on airs — in this case literally by liberally applying perfume.

Doug, 39, Phoenix

Whores tend to overdo all feminine signals (i.e. dress and makeup) and also are often thought to be dirty. Since the French are considered dirtier and smellier by those of British descent, it follows that a French whore would be particularly smelly, indeed.

Tara, Morgantown, W.Va.

We found:

We can sometimes offend particular groups of people, so let's be clear: We in no way wish to affront prostitutes.

They do dally in sex, though, and sexual daring is what the French are often associated with, said Scott P. Sheridan, associate

36

professor at Illinois Wesleyan University who studies French culture and has even listed "Decadence" as a professional interest.

What you have here are historical truisms getting meshed with stereotypes, he said.

For one thing, as far back as at least the 19th century, France was noted for being a more sexually open culture, especially compared with our Puritanical ways. American GIs in World Wars I and II then regaled friends stateside with tales of pretty, hospitable and pretty hospitable French prostitutes.

Now add in some stereotypes, Sheridan said: The French don't bathe much (they do, but aren't as obsessive as Americans) and douse themselves in perfume to cover body odor (we're talking Napoleonic era with that one).

Mix everything together, and you get an image of sweaty prostitutes who carry a certain bouquet and then heap on the eau de toilette to hide it.

The danger in all this is that Americans, who've pretty much caught up to western Europe in promiscuity, hold onto these images and assume they are somehow "better" or more moral than the French.

"France has become one of the few countries it's still OK to bash," Sheridan said. "It's still a punching bag for stereotypes because we assume the French aren't relevant anymore."

Sheesh, no wonder they're so rude to us.

Who says all the smokin' models are imported?

They asked:

How come the hottest-looking models are always from foreign countries?

Roland, 15, Fleming Island

You said:

Supply and demand. Import vs. domestic. In a purely market-driven economy, even the hot models are more attractive simply because they come from somewhere other than America. Truthfully, the foreign models are quite hideous and must be air-brushed to hide the multiple flaws. The term "coyote ugly" applies to models from other countries.

Spartan80, 44, female, Texas

It's probably because most models you see are from the Victoria's Secret Angels "team." We have had plenty of American supermodels: Tyra Banks, Cindy Crawford, Niki Taylor, Kim Alexis, Rebecca Romijn, etc. One reason it may seem there are so many foreign-born models is that the fashion capitals of the world are primarily in Europe . . . .

Nicole, 22, Jacksonville

Maybe they just seem hot to you because they look more exotic than corn-fed U.S. models. I'm not sure what those foreign beauties eat — not much? I do think the foreign models look a bit different since they tend to have a certain ethnic look vs. U.S. models, who are often a combination of many nationalities. Kinda like a purebred vs. a mutt.

Buford, 43, Adamsville, Tenn.

We found:

Roland, meet Kim Alexis. Well, probably in your dreams, but at least we can introduce you via the printed word.

"You're probably looking in the wrong place," Alexis says she'd tell you if you posed your question in the flesh.

The former supermodel says that yes, Victoria's Secret and magazines like Maxim mean there are more chances for models willing to show more skin to do just that.

"Some girls in other countries are raised with a more liberal outlook on their body and what they will do with their body," said Alexis, who now counsels girls considering modeling to "be careful about doing anything that makes you feel uncomfortable or violated."

"I suppose there's 'hot' and then there's 'beautiful.' And there are beautiful girls all over the world," she said. "Sometimes young boys don't care about beauty."

Real beauty to her is a classic, fresh look, not gaunt and haunted, as is the fad lately.

Stylist Darleen Unger of the Northeast Florida chapter of Fashion Group International would agree, and adds that Roland might be thinking he's seeing "exotic" models when in fact they may hail from Alabama or Chicago.

"The other thing is that Armani and other European designers now hold shows in New York, and years ago they didn't do that.

"They will bring models with them, so you have a chance to see these foreign models whereas perhaps in the past you didn't."

Will you stop touching my belly?

Since I've been pregnant with my first child, complete strangers come up to me and rub my belly. Why do people think this is socially acceptable?

Tracy, 25, Jacksonville

You said:

Some people are not socially educated. While I was pregnant, people found joy in knowing of the miracle of life growing inside. That elicits an urge to take part in that joy. Although people you don't know shouldn't approach you and rub your belly without asking, hopefully you can understand that they must be happy for you.

Cyndi, 41, Stoneville, Miss.

My son is 14 months now. When I was pregnant, not many people touched my belly without asking. My friends and I talked about this very subject, and some said a lot of people did touch their bellies and some said they did not. So it is my opinion that maybe it is the personality of the pregnant woman that may draw strangers to touch their bellies.

Susan R., 29, Cleveland, Miss.

We found:

People pat pregnant paunches for several reasons, says Paula Spencer Scott (paulaspencerscott.com), author of "Everything Else You Need to Know When You're Expecting" (Griffin):

Folks are just damn glad to see laden ladies.

"They're excited about the prospect of a baby . . . they forget themselves in their enthusiasm," said Spencer Scott, who writes the Momfidence! column for Woman's Day magazine.

They want to bear . . . your . . . children (well, not exactly).

"People want to vicariously participate in the pregnancy. They can't carry the baby for you, but they can pat it."

They're amazed.

"They've just never been close to a belly. And in today's fashion world, we're flaunting that belly like it's an irresistible, exotic fruit."

They think they'll hit the jackpot if they brush that breadbasket.

"Some odd souls consider it good luck, like rubbing the lucky Buddha."

What's a glowing gal to do or say? According to Spencer Scott:

Realize most people aren't trying to be rude. "They are thinking they are touching your baby, not your body."

Have a good comeback. "If somebody says they can't resist a pregnant belly, say, 'Yes, but it's attached to my body.' "

Make like you're sick. Really sick. "One line I've heard is, 'It makes me nauseous when people do that.' Believe me, no one wants to go there."

Head for the potty. "That's a good one if it's becoming a group grope."

Know your internal sense of what crosses the line, and use a sliding scale for offenders. "Probably your male boss is on one end, and your partner is on the other."

Here's the 411 on strippers and 420

They asked:

Why are so many strippers into dope?

Deanna, 27, Irvine, Calif.

You said:

I think the reason they do drugs is to numb themselves from the humiliation of having men act disgusting around them.

Dwanny, 51, female, Fort Worth

I have been in the exotic dancer business for nine years; most of the girls are actually in college, or they are supporting their families. It's not all about drugs. I won't lie to you; it is all about the money.

Mary, Austin, Texas

I think some dancers use drugs for the same reasons other people use drugs: escape, not thinking about the future, inability to resist temptation, to be cool. Dancers (we don't really use stripper that much) tend to do OK with money, and it is cash, so maybe they have more access or opportunity. Generally the girls at the better clubs don't as much as the girls at the not-so-nice clubs — not sure what is cause and what is effect, because once you start abusing drugs (including alcohol) regularly, it's usually a slide down to the bottom.

Kiana, 37, dancer, Atlanta

We found:

Stripped to its bare essence, this is really about whether someone can drink alcohol and smoke pot and still maintain their pole position.

Viewed from that angle (or multiple angles, if you prefer), exotic dancer expert Bernadette Barton (bernadettebarton.com) says yes, they can — to an extent.

"Dancers are encouraged to drink on the job; the boss and the customers want them to drink. They don't want them so intoxicated that they can't function, but just enough to loosen them up. The more they drink, the more money they make," said Barton, a Morehead State University sociology professor who researched dancers for 12 years and wrote "Stripped: Inside the Lives of Exotic Dancers."

Because they are usually working in a bar to begin with, there's more access to alcohol and marijuana, Barton noted.

"One dancer I interviewed said it was typical for the 'pot guy' to come into the club, the 'cocaine guy' to come into the club . . . you probably won't get that in your accounting office," Barton said.

Because sex work can take a toll on a person over time — with rude and abusive customers, intrusive touching, insults, poor relationships, jealous partners, a stigma that encourages hiding the work, and even a reduced sex drive and general disdain for men that can develop — it can cause mounting pressures that lead to abusing drugs or alcohol.

It's important not to demonize them, she stressed.

"We as a society are all doped up: People are on caffeine, anti-depressants, sleeping pills, drinking six-packs when they get home," she said. "As a culture we use a lot of drugs, because we have a difficult work world right now."

That world has not exactly put strippers in the lap-dance of luxury lately.

"The economy is ... affecting dancers, and not in a good way," Barton said.

"It's harder to make the same amount of money. There's more sexual labor involved, and they have to push it more. . . . The women who end up remaining exotic dancers might be those most vulnerable, those who are most addicted. I'm speculating, but it could be that the percent of the dancer population on dope may be increasing because of the economy."

Why are Susie's toys so wimpy?

They asked:

I can't help noticing the difference between girls' and boys' toys. It's pathetic. All girls' toys center on mothering, dressing or cute crafts. In the boys' corner you get monsters, machines, game stations and challenging games. Any thoughts?

T., 32, female, Germany

You said:

The reason for this is that children are being socialized to accept the positions they are expected to fulfill in later life.

Deborah, 23, Miss.

If girls want to play with boys' toys, they have serious problems and should be sent to a good protocol school. Ideally, I'd like young women to wear gloves in public and actually appreciate it when men are holding doors for them, etc.

C.C., 22, Canada

C.C., I grew up on He-Man, ThunderCats and Transformers and turned out normal. You?

Sarah, 24, San Francisco

As a child, if I wanted a toy it was because it looked fun, not because it was a girl's toy or a boy's toy — and that is what we should teach girls today.

Nydia, 16, Houston

Feminist nonsense aside, there are real differences between males and females. Toy companies are not perpetrating some evil patriarchal conspiracy on little girls.

J.F., 60, male, Dayton, Ohio

All little boys should wear dresses and learn to braid their hair and the proper way to use a tampon, as little girls should be given a BB gun and taught how to shoot the neighbor's cat and the proper way to put on a condom and pee on a tree. Because there ain't no difference between them — is there?

John S., 20, Conn.

I was in love with that Barbie crap. But I also liked my cousin's Snot Factory, G.I. Joe and Creepy Crawlers. Yes, the world's youth are being subjugated to gender-based differences, but they're still going to play with what they want.

Kayt, 14, Greenwich, Conn.

We found:

Picture C.C. and John S. on a play-date together as children. That's all we're saying about it.

Also, picture Texas A&M University researcher Gerianne Alexander (geriannealexander.com) watching monkeys play with toys. She does it a lot.

She and fellow researchers found that girl monkeys play more with girlie toys like dolls, and boy monkeys play more with boy-toys like balls.

"Socialization plays a role in toy selection, but there is a role for biological factors, too."

So why Johnny often likes a gun and Susie a rag doll may be partly due to hormones. Studies have speculated that for survival of the species, females may be innately programmed for nurturing, and males for motion or rough play.

"Toy companies like Mattel do a lot of market research," Alexander said. "They aren't just pushing toys . . . they actually look at who plays with what."

In fact, Mattel markets Polly Pocket Polly Wheels — though there are distinct differences in how these "girlie cars" are marketed.

"They are for racing to the mall," Alexander noted.

Most girls aren't neigh-sayers about horses

They asked:

I am a man who loves horses. Yet it seems that more than 80 percent of the people involved in horsemanship are women (mainly teenage girls). Why?

Robert, 34, Birmingham

You said:

Horse-loving women ponder this, too. You'd think men interested in meeting women would gravitate to horses, but instead they seem to prefer NASCAR. I do think horses represent a fantasy that can be made real — the special friendship, the freedom of riding and the camaraderie of other women who like being around horses, too.

Anne M., Albuquerque, N.M.

Maybe there's just something about having something so large and muscular between your legs that we mortal men could never match (sigh).

Mike, Richmond, Va.

I call it "the big doll" theory: Before you go riding, you have to groom the horse and clean his hooves, etc. Then you dress him up in his saddle, blanket and bridle and all. It's like playing Barbies on a very large scale.

P.J., California

Women seldom get the experience of moving fast and having 1,000 pounds of steel-shod muscle under the command of their slightest shift in weight. It makes us feel free and graceful. You thought it was going to be some kinky sex thing, didn't you?

Elaine C., Columbus, Ohio

We found:

A horse is a horse . . . of course, of course!

Really, writer Vicky Moon (vickymoon.com) of horse mecca Middleburg, Va., says, there's nothing hot about riding a giant, hoofed mammal.

"When all you're thinking about is 'Please, dear God, let me stay on,' you're not thinking about anything sensual," said Moon, author of "A Sunday Horse" and "The Private Passion of Jackie Kennedy Onassis: Portrait of A Rider."

And while lots of young girls are into horses, at the highest levels of equestrianism — the Olympics, horse-jumping, horse-racing, polo — it's men who still dominate, she said. But about that gender disparity at the lower levels: Moon likes the "control" and "doll" theories.

"Horses are big, friendly and easily intimidated. Here you are a little girl, and it gives you confidence to take care of, ride and control a big horse," she said.

"As far as it being like a big doll, it's true. It's a nurturing thing. You have it from a little age. To this day I love to give horses a bath. It's very caring."

Shrewd fathers who steer their young sons toward baseball or football should consider horsemanship, she added. Polo players can make tens of thousands of dollars a week.

And yes, it's a good way to rub shoulders with women.

"My son loved it for that reason: to meet girls. It's a chick-magnet thing."

Are spiked heels and tight tees really for little girls?

They asked:

Why do families I see at the mall or movies dress their little girls in clothes not appropriate to their age group? Like high heels, short-shorts and tight T-shirts that say things like "Cherry" or "Your Boyfriend Wants Me"?

Clare, 27, Jacksonville

You said:

What ticks me off is "tweens" wearing tiny shorts with the writing on the seat. Or worse, shirts with the writing at chest level. It's the last place a 12-year-old should be drawing attention to.

Brad, 32, Winchester, Va.

I have three kids — two of them are girls. And I would beat that shit if they ever walked out of my house like that.

Rainn, 23, Waynesboro, Va.

Rainn, I hope before you start beating your children for dressing like that you will first talk to them in a loving (and firm) manner. Educate them verbally without resorting to causing them physical pain because they want to do what teenagers do: rebel!

Marie, New York, N.Y.

In a better society, kids could wear what they wanted and not be sexualized by people.

Dina M., Chicago

Manufacturers are selling these sexy clothes because they know the little girls want them. All little girls want to do is be like the older girls — or their moms.

Emily, 30, Shelby, Miss.

We found:

Humor columnist and New York Times best-selling author Celia Rivenbark (celiarivenbark.com), author of such books as "Stop Dressing Your Six-Year-Old Like a Skank" and "Rude Bitches Make Me Tired," says she noticed the "prosti-tot" trend really take hold in the early 2000s. While many might point to Britney Spears or even Hilary Duff as the provocateurs of little girls who now ache to dress suggestively, Rivenbark says think Bratz dolls and the Cheetah Girls TV show and you're closer to the real culprits.

"The Cheetah Girls are part of the Disney stable, so you'd think it's OK, but they wear ho clothes. And little girls see this and want to emulate the belly shirts, fishnet stockings and very short skirts."

Then there are the Bratz dolls, which Rivenbark says are "made on purpose to look like tiny little streetwalkers."

"Go and look at Toys 'R' Us. You'll faint. And this is the doll of choice of 7-year-old girls."

Beyond the obvious danger of attracting potential molesters with T-shirts that read "Made You Look," there's the problem of sexualizing children well before their time, to the point they miss out on childhood and jump into sexual activity much too soon, she said.

Moms and dads who placate their whining kids at the clothes shop had better think twice, added Rivenbark, who has a 9-year-old daughter.

"We have a huge problem saying no to our kids. I don't know if it's misplaced guilt at not spending enough time with them or what."

She has a simple solution if her own daughter gets too pushy about clothes, though.

"I'm the mommy, not the friend. I say NO. If she keeps on, I say HELL NO!"

Keeping abreast of flat-chested swimmers

They asked:

Do female swimmers have small breasts because they swim, or do they swim because they have small breasts?

Kyle and Cody, 15, Clay County

You said:

Top female swimmers swim because they have small breasts. Certain sports are conducive to different body shapes. Also, if some male swimmers go so far as to shave their heads to better their times by fractions of a second, then double-D breasts would definitely slow someone down.

Renea, Orange Park

A young woman once told me her breasts were the first place she lost weight upon embarking on a physical fitness program. She saw it as cruel injustice, since that part of her body was the one area she was satisfied with. This suggests that an avid swimmer might indeed lose fatty but fabulous breast tissue over the course of many laps.

Thomas, 43, Wheaton, Ill.

Spandex, long known for its low resistance to water friction, is worn very tight for maximum speed, thus smushing the breasts. Also, breasts are largely made up of fat, and successful swimmers are lean, so it's both. Then there is the boring answer of lesser resistance through the water with small breasts — unlike the spoiler on a '68 'Cuda.

Joe, 45, Illinois

We found:

We can't help being impressed with Nancy Hogshead-Makar: Three-time Olympic gold medal swimmer. Title IX expert, attorney and former law professor. Senior Director of Advocacy for the Women's Sports Foundation.

Doesn't slam the phone down when asked about swimmers' breasts.

"Most top swimmers with bigger breasts tend to compete in the backstroke because . . ."

Now, right about here, she paused and pondered how best to continue. We helped.

"Because it would create more drag in the pool if they swam face-down?"

"Something like that," she said.

Overall, though, swimmers come in all shapes, Hogshead-Makar said. Their breasts don't get smaller from working out (they're made of breast tissue and fatty tissue, so getting leaner won't necessarily "spot-reduce" them).

As well, larger shoulders from weight-training can create the illusion of smaller breasts on a female swimmer, she said.

While it's true that too much training can stunt a young swimmer's growth and even slow puberty, it hinders performance overall, so trainers try not to over-train athletes.

And even though a sleeker body can be better aerodynamically, that doesn't mean only small-breasted women swim.

"There are a lot of 'normal'-looking top female swimmers, but our culture has become used to thinking that 'normal' women have big breasts, from TV and magazines. So when they see a normal woman swimming, they might think she has small breasts," Hogshead-Makar said.

"It used to be that there was nothing embarrassing about looking average."

Oral arguments for and against tongue piercing

They asked:

I have a tongue piercing. In all other respects I look conventional. What would your reaction be if you saw me?

Anne, 19, London

You said:

What runs through my head is "ow!" I grew up in the San Francisco Bay Area, and it got to the point that if you didn't have multiple piercings and tattoos, people would look at you oddly.

Doug, 39, Phoenix

I'd think there's some lucky dentist out there who's going to be driving a fancy sports car some day off your teeth. Hope you're keeping an eye on denture ads; you will be wearing them.

Steve, 46, Houston

I would suspect you're kinkier than average.

Lee, 26, male, United Kingdom

I wish I could say it doesn't bother me at all, but it does. If I were a hiring manager with two identical candidates, one pierced and the other not, which one do you think I would hire?

Dave, 48, Bristol, Conn.

I never judge people with piercings as troublesome or lawbreakers. It has nothing to do with character. Employers in general refuse to hire anyone with body piercings, which shouldn't be an issue if it's in moderation.

Monique, Fort Myers

Fifteen years ago I would have thought: "Cool. She must be a bad-ass." Now I think, "Fashion takes every authentic statement and renders it pointless."

J., 34, female, Chicago

When I see women with pierced tongues, I assume they are promiscuous. When I see men with pierced tongues, I assume they are promiscuous and homosexual.

Nik, 24, female, San Francisco

We found:

Is a tongue-lashing in order here? Not really, says Victoria Pitts, sociology professor at the City University of New York and author of "In the Flesh: The Cultural Politics of Body Modification" and "Surgery Junkies: Wellness and Pathology in Cosmetic Culture."

While youths often get tongue piercings to feel unique, in reality they are just following cultural trends — even as they hope to send a message that they reject mainstream culture.

"They are trying to express their individuality, but the irony is that . . . when we mark our bodies, we are doing something about connectedness, because we are acknowledging how our bodies are social spaces that are read by others," said Pitts.

No, it doesn't help at job interview time, but most youths don't hang onto fads long and move on to something else, anyway, she noted.

That's one reason tongue piercings don't pose much of a health risk: They're removable and generally not worn for long periods.

As far as people with tongue piercings being more interested in sex or sexual foreplay, Pitts said that's nonsense.

"Men in particular like to sexualize certain areas of the body, including the tongue. But there's no legitimacy to that argument."

This question just cuts way too close

They asked:

I understand female circumcision is mandatory in many Middle East countries. Is it practiced in the United States and other non-Muslim countries?

Jerry, 63, Catholic, Marco Island

You said:

"Female circumcision" is actually genital mutilation. It is not common in Western countries. It leaves the woman virtually unable to enjoy sexual intercourse and usually makes it a painful and frightening experience.

J. McLain, 46, Christian male, Middleburg

Islam frowns very much upon this practice. In the Koran where sexual relations between husband and wife are discussed, it is made clear that a man must make it his priority to (completely) satisfy his wife before he himself is satisfied. This clearly would go against any such butchering of the female body that would prevent her from attaining intimate release.

Jen H., 19, Muslim, Clark, N.J.

I'm an OB-GYN, so I've seen a fair bit of this. It is done here but not too commonly, and in secret. Most people have it done to their daughters before moving to the United States, or on trips home.

Deborah, 37, Fairfield, Calif.

No one in my family has received a female circumcision. In some African tribes, this is a ritual, but nowhere in Islam does it mention this topic.

Mariam, Muslim, Arlington, Va.

This is a cultural practice attributed to Islam to provide religious justification for its continuation.

Glenn, 48, Christian, Turkey

We found:

Female Genital Cutting, or FGC (many women who've undergone it dislike the term Female Genital Mutilation) may have its roots in ancient Egypt. Nowadays it's mostly performed in 28 African and a few Middle Eastern countries, on up to 2 million girls a year between ages 4 and 12, according to the World Health Organization. It's not mandated and is illegal in many of these places, but some governments look the other way.

The stated reasons for it? It's a "good tradition;" a "cultural norm;" a "rite of passage;" it "qualifies" a woman for wifehood; "enhances male sexuality;" "curbs female sexual desire;" "preserves virginity."

You'll notice "it's a Muslim thing" isn't listed; there's nothing in the sacred text of any major religion that prescribes FGC. But it's been a cultural practice for so long in some parts of the world that some Muslims and Christians mistakenly believe it's a religious requirement, said Laura Katzive, former deputy director of the International Legal Program of the Center for Reproductive Rights and now program officer for human rights philanthropic firm Wellspring Advisors.

"The major leaders in the Muslim community have even said it's not called for by Islam."

Because of immigration from other countries, the Centers for Disease Control says up to 160,000 girls in the U.S. are at risk for the procedure. There's a federal law against it, and 17 states, including Georgia, have banned it.

Remember that chick who rocked her legs in class?

They asked:

I have noticed that women seated with crossed legs frequently rhythmically move their top leg up and down, or alternatively pivot their foot. Are they just nervous, or is there something, shall we say, more interesting going on?

Peter N., Madison, Wis.

You said:

No, your fantasies aren't true.

Anna B., 52, Seattle

Is everything sex to men? It's just fidgeting. And, to let you know a little secret, foot-twirling burns something like 250 calories an hour. That's why I twirl my feet when I sit cross-legged. Also, sitting cross-legged isn't exceptionally comfortable for extended periods of time if you don't move your legs.

Yvonne, 27, Columbia, Mo.

I pivot my foot, and it's just something that relaxes me. I'm gonna be a bit more conscious of it now, oh dear!

Milly, London

If we could get something more out of it, we might do it more.

Katrina, 21, Moses Lake, Wash.

Pete, is there anything, anything else at all, that might have caught your attention over all those years up in Wisconsin?

Ron S., 60, Stockton, Calif.

We found:

Sorry, guys. Sixty-six out of 66 women responders can't be wrong: It's leg-bobbing. Not masturbating.

"It's likely anxiety of some kind, or they [leg-bobbers] are lost in thought, just as you might run your fingers through your hair or tap your fingers on the table," says acclaimed California sexologist Lonnie Barbach (lonniebarbach.com), author of numerous books including "The Erotic Edge" and "For Yourself: The Fulfillment of Female Sexuality."

If anything, she said, this question says less about women than it does men, who aren't known to allow much time to elapse before enjoying a carnal thought (though, contrary to a myth attributed to sex researcher Alfred Kinsey, it's not once every seven seconds, but more like 37 times a week, compared to nine for women, a California State University study recently revealed).

"Maybe men are just keeping their erotic lives fresh by thinking this," Barbach said with a laugh. "I mean, isn't that an interesting fantasy?"

To get to the details: such public leg movement just doesn't do anything to contract a woman's thigh muscles — which is a pretty critical part of the precise scenario that would involve a women pleasuring herself.

"When women are in public, they're in public," Barbach said. "While you guys are fantasizing about what we're doing, we're busy doing other things."

Sometimes a woman sans panties is just ... comfortable

They asked:

I have "gone commando" (no underwear) for a few years. When I suggest it to other women to prevent yeast infections and for comfort, they think it is slutty or that I must be "secretly kinky." Has anyone else run into this stupidity?

Rina, 22, Royal Palm Beach

You said:

I haven't worn underwear in about two years. It's better for you. Less bacteria, less infections, etc. I think it's worse for girls to have thongs hangin' out of their pants. That's trashy.

Jen, 23, Mattapoisett, Mass.

I, too, have gone commando. When I reached adulthood it was my first official act. There is nothing wrong with not wearing underwear. We're too restrictive as a society. Why should your underwear, or lack thereof, reveal secrets about your moral worth?

Kevin, 35, Jacksonville

If men can do it, why can't we? I have a few friends who do it, and they are not perverted. I don't, only because it is uncomfortable, as I wear mainly jeans and they can chafe. I have a teen daughter who is a virgin, and she is comfy going "bare down there," and I would never think of her as a whore or slutty.

Reesa, 37, Ellensburg, Wash.

I have to wonder why you think it's all right to suggest something as intensely personal as going without underwear to your friends. If a friend were to tell me that, I'd be somewhat offended. Perhaps you should stay away from sharing such intimate details of your life.

Melody, 40, Kansas City, Mo.

I went through a long phase of going commando. Maybe I was missing out on some side benefit, but I certainly wasn't out there being promiscuous.

Emily, 29, Syracuse, N.Y.

The perception that because you have one less layer for a man to remove to get your "goods" that you must be sexually promiscuous is typical of the Puritan mentality that affects this country.

Ann, 37, Kansas City, Mo.

We found:

With National Underwear Day every Aug. 5 getting more and more popular (hundreds now celebrate in their skivvies in Times Square), we felt it important to discuss those in the minority who don't cotton to wearing them.

Of 20,000 responses to a survey by undergarment retailer Freshpair.com, 25 percent of men preferred boxers, 32 percent briefs, 28 percent boxer briefs, 4 percent thongs (yikes), 4 percent "other styles" and 7 percent nothing. Among women, 49 percent prefer panties, 28 percent thongs, 13 percent "boyshorts," 4 percent "other styles" and 6 percent nothing.

Most who go commando don't do so out of wanton depravity, says Michael Kleinmann, former president of Freshpair.com, who started National Underwear Day in 2003 to promote more recognition of the so-called "unmentionables."

"When people don't wear underwear, the reason is for comfort, or they don't want underwear lines," said Kleinmann, founder of UnderwearExpert.com. "It's typically in the summer."

Whether you do or don't, be glad it's not 1933 — the year before the world's first truly functional vent was installed in boxers and briefs.

The O.U.T.L.O.U.D. Method to Dialogue

OPEN UP: This is mostly about opening up to yourself. Why do you want to engage someone? Is it for the right reasons? The answers might help you figure out how to approach another person. A friend once told me the real reason I started Y? wasn't for me to learn more about "Buddhists in Asia or lesbians in San Francisco," but because I wanted to learn something more about myself. He was right. Acknowledging that has helped give me perspective when considering others' answers.

USE YOUR HEAD: Plan for the right question. Not all questions need to be the "wet dogs" variety. Stereotypes and clichés don't work as well as sincere attempts to talk.

TIME IT RIGHT: Create the "O.U.T.L.O.U.D. Moment". Pick your spots for provocative dialogue. Find a genuine opening rather than create a false one. It's often during those down times between all the "vital" discourse that we can most easily find a direct path to someone's point of view. If you spend enough time sitting in the cubicle next to someone of a different culture, chances are there'll come a time — over food, perhaps, or during a power outage — when the topic you've been dying to broach will wend its way naturally into the discussion.

LOCK IN ON THE TARGET: Keeping things simple can give the best chance for getting another's trust and a meaningful reply. Some of the best questions at Y?, those that prompt the most telling answers, are also often the easiest to digest. Remember, it's not about winning your point. It's what comes from the heart that counts most — and captures people's interest. Talking from the heart also means easing into things by letting someone know *why* it would help you to learn the answer to your question before you ask it.

OWN UP TO ASSUMPTIONS: One of the most refreshing and repetitive surprises of the Y? project is the difficulty in predicting how a person will respond to a question. Blacks do not think in lockstep. Nor do whites. Nor Christians or Muslims. Nor gays or straights. Be receptive to another's ideas. Wipe the slate clean and listen to the content of the message, not the color or culture of the messenger.

UNLOAD YOUR EXPECTATIONS: Many of us are thinner-skinned than we'll admit. When we get hit with an answer or comment we hadn't anticipated, our emotions can often get caught off-balance, and our egos get bruised. The solution: Expect the unexpected. You'll never be blindsided or taken aback by information that doesn't gibe with your worldview.

DIGEST THE DIALOGUE: Learning about others doesn't stop when the talking's over. Assess what you're told and how it fits with or departs from your perspectives. Recap your discussion with a third party to distill the most relevant information into its most meaningful points.

ABOUT THE AUTHOR

Phillip J. Milano is the founder of Y? The National Forum on People's Differences, the acclaimed cross-cultural dialogue project that encourages people to ask unflinching, politically incorrect questions about our differences.

Since its creation in 1998, Phillip's web site, YForum.com, has attracted millions of visitors and thousands of questions and answers. He has been featured on CBS, CNN, BET and the BBC, and in numerous newspapers, including The Washington Post, New York Times and USA Today.

He is the author of the Perigee book "I Can't Believe You Asked That!" as well as writer of the pioneering newspaper column/blog "Dare to Ask."

Mr. Milano is a 25-year newspaper veteran. He received his Master of Business Administration from Northern Illinois University and his Bachelor of Science in Journalism from Southern Illinois University.

SPEECHES AND APPEARANCES

Mr. Milano is an in-demand speaker. For bookings, contact

Contemporary Issues Agency
809 Turnberry Drive, Waunakee, WI 53597-2256
Phone: 800-843-2179
Fax: 608-849-6311
www.CIAspeakers.com
Info@CIAspeakers.com